Mahogany Soul Rise
For You Are The Sacred Word

Mahogany Soul Rise
For You Are The Sacred Word

Written By Dana Rondel

What Inspiration Sounds and Looks Like
www.partnersingoodwill.com

Copyright © 2010 by Dana Rondel
Published by Partners In Goodwill 2014 (Revised Edition),
Metaphors 4 Life 2010
Cover Design by Partners In Goodwill
Cover Image by Dana Rondel

All rights reserved. No part of this book may be reproduced by any mechanical, photographic, or electronic process, or in the form of a phonographic recording; nor may it be stored in a retrieval system, transmitted, or otherwise be copied for public or private use — other than for "fair use" as brief quotations embodied in articles and reviews —without prior written permission of the publisher. The intent of the author is only to offer information that will hopefully broaden your knowledge and perspective regarding the content being shared. In the event you use any of the information in this book for personal or professional reasons, which is your constitutional right, the author and the publisher assume no responsibility for your actions.

ISBN: 978-0-9817291-5-2
ISBN: 0-9817291-5-0

This book is printed on acid-free paper. Printed in the United States of America.

But when the work was finished, the Craftsman kept wishing that there were someone to ponder the plan of so great a work, to love its beauty, and to wonder at its vastness. Therefore, when everything was done... He finally took thought concerning the creation of man... He therefore took man as a creature of indeterminate nature and, assigning him a place in the middle of the world, addressed him thus: "Neither a fixed abode nor a form that is thine alone nor any function peculiar to thyself have we given thee, Adam, to the end that according to thy longing and according to thy judgement thou mayest have and possess what abode, what form and what functions thou thyself shalt desire. The nature of all other beings is limited and constrained within the bounds of law. Thou shalt have the power to degenerate into the lower forms of life, which are brutish. Thou shalt have the power, out of thy soul's judgement, to be born into the higher forms, which are divine."

(Pico 224-225)

See what is before you and know that this creation was born from the very Soul that, too, gave birth to you...

And the Word became flesh, and dwelt among us, and we saw His glory, glory as of the only begotten from the Father, full of grace and truth.

- John 1:14

A special thanks to every man who lives, for you live for me too...

Father, you gave of yourself, and received in return the brilliance of God...a gift...to bring light into the world...

In the beginning was The Word...

Inside

Inside

The tears of our tumultuous past are those that had formed stormy oceans. We, the human family, had witnessed with our eyes the downtrodden souls of our Earth's beloved sons. Our tears had fallen down from the murky skies of our internal souls and met the water of our first Mother, causing her to weep too... We had stood before her feeling helpless. It seemed we could not find the means within us to catch our brethrens' tears to wash our men clean again, before their tears could fall into the abyss of eternity. If only the fluid substance that emanated from our collective pain had welled up in the palms of our hands, us, your mothers', sisters', daughters', Queens, and made a river, rather than pour through our nimble fingers and escape us, perhaps then we, too, could've watered properly that flower that pressed to blossom within you, our noble brothers...

We Looked

We Looked

As we looked upon the face of our fathers, our brothers, our sons, Black Kings in the land of our primitive Mother, we wondered what was it that our men saw in their own eyes; what words planted themselves in their minds; what feelings numbed their hearts; what touch exploited their souls and compelled them to let go of and shun the beautiful Black body He, our God, is in? That he, your father, is in? Through blood, bones and colored skin, we heard the afflicted voice expressing itself and screaming out: I am not Him/him! But it was only the voice that spoke through exterior reflections...

After

After

After being birthed into life, somewhere on the path of living our brethren seemed to lose their true Selves. They seemed to no longer accept that God was alive in them...*God is alive in him*...a notion of long ago ages, of those who were wiser than us, whose teachings now urge us to acknowledge this truth again...*God is alive in him*... For if man comes to fully know Him, root and branch, he would find that he is above all earthly things, invincible, yet still in the world...living in accord with Spirit, Nature and Man. True Love has finally helped him to find his way back to this truth—God is everywhere...including inside of him...

We Are One

We Are One

We are one with each other, woman and man, of the same Divine body, yet although this be true, it was you, our brethren who had to reach down into the depths of your own souls to grasp that thing that oppressed you. It was you who had to let it go... Those of us, your mothers, sisters, daughters, Queens, who could not accept your lifelessness, then pulled you back into us to breathe into you again love and courage...and therefore love and courage and strength came alive inside of you once more, and they gave power and life to the arms beside you...that awaited your command...to be lifted up, stretched out and pushed down into the flesh and soul of your being, so that your strong and worthy hands could pull away and clear the oppressor of your mind and heart...

If You Will

If You Will

If you, our brethren, could not find the strength to make yourselves free again, then that stranger within you would have become your voiceless shadow. We, your mothers, sisters, daughters, Queens, heard your fever's cry, though faint. We saw for ourselves, through wisdom's eye, the pangs that stabbed you on the inside and made you bow to their mercy. We saw what others may not have. We knew your insatiable hunger and thirst for liberation and love. We, too, starved and longed for liberation and love, and therefore, we chose freedom for ourselves and for you: Your desires, our brethren, were not meant to be silenced. They were meant to be spoken into words, sung into song, written into poetry and brought into being by living truth. Life is the ultimate path to truth, but so many of you, fathers, brothers, sons, our Kings, willingly held tightly on to death, afraid to let it go, because for so long you remembered death not as a deceptive and cunning foe, but as a loving friend who suckled and comforted you...

Death

Death

Death, like you, our brethren, is dark. So it fooled you into believing that it was your only reflection. The shadow lured you deeper and deeper into itself; it cradled you in its bosom and gently caressed your brow while compelling you into a sound and perpetual sleep. But life didn't give up on you; it beckoned to you to awake and rise from your lifeless trance and live...so that you might again become your *God-Self*.

Who was the perpetrator who tried to separate Him from you? Who tried to separate him from you? Who tried to take from you, our brethren, the knowing that reminded you all of you, the Man? What intruder caused you to warily release your grasp from what was yours and only yours to give—your heart, mind, body and spirit? Whoever and whatever it was had, too, taken you from us, your mothers, sisters, daughters, Queens. We all knew that in time, you, our brethren, would have given your complete self freely to us all, but in the right way. You each knew this even as a child, because the voice of God spoke to you all then too. But later as men you each knew because of the guilt and shame that constantly reminded you. Finally, you let them go, guilt and shame, and moved toward another time, another place, another you and called forth that which was taken from you, and opened your arms to receive, embrace and love your life back into wholeness—Selves that are the highest of you.

You Are

You Are

Shall She/she, mothers of you, who birthed you into the world, be the first to grow you into men? Shall She/she be the first to expose your nakedness to the mirror that, when looked into, allows you to see the full truth of who you are? Shall She/she be the first to remind you that you are more than man, and that you resemble her first love, God? Shall She/she be the first to raise you above your earthly self, so that you can know more of yourself? Shall She/she be the first to teach you that you have always been and will always be the greatest gift of life and love? Shall She/she be the first to call you by His/his name?

You are a reflection of Him, your Father...of him, your fathers. Will it be Him/him who teaches you how to grow into men? Shall He/he teach you by his walk how to love self, so that you, too, can walk with your head held high, your back straight, your shoulders broad, your chest commanding and your eyes affectionate, still and directly looking into ours, women? Shall He/he show you that your hands were made to mold mountains, dig valleys and clear paths for our footsteps, your Queens, in order that we might make a way for our children to follow? Shall He/he assist you in discovering that Kings are entitled to Queens and that only they together can build villages, nations and worlds? Shall He/he create for you the image of what it means to be a Man? Will you let Him/him?

Words

Words

Words are given power when conceived in our minds and uttered through our lips. In the beginning God made a sound and sound became words and words became Creation. Woman, she speaks and the light of the world comes forth... Man, he speaks and the light of the world comes forth... Woman and Man, they speak and the world itself comes forth... Words are given power when conceived in our minds and uttered through our lips. If we, too, are gods and our words have the power to bring forth brighter worlds, what then manifests when we live by and speak from love? We have the power to create and build Man and the World...

I AM, We Are

I AM, We Are

I AM, We Are... I am, We are Her/her. You are Her/her. I am, We are Him/him. You are Him/him. I am, We are, gotten from you and you from me and we from Them...Woman...Man...We are the same but, too, we are different, for I am her, your mother, sister, daughter, Queen....And you are him, my father, brother, son, King.... *I am because you are and you are because I am and We Are because S/He is...* I exist...I am Woman. We exist...We are Woman and Man... You exist...You are Man...

All that I really want to say is...S/He is Me and You and We, who I love...with words... and beyond words...

Now, Father, glorify Me together with Yourself, with the glory which I had with You before the world was.

- *John 17:5*

...who, although He existed in the form of God, did not regard equality with God a thing to be grasped...

- *Philippians 2:6*

He is clothed with a robe dipped in blood, and His name is called The Word of God...

- *Revelations 19:13*

Omniversal Life International (OLI) Life and Leadership

Omniversal Life International (OLI) provides the necessary training, tools and wisdom to become a wiser and happier individual as well as a renowned leader in the professional world. Our leaders, those who have been trained within the OLI Life & Leadership Program, have the capacity to guide others toward outcomes that allow for healthier relationships, greater personal and professional growth and higher tangible returns. What makes *Omniversal Life International (OLI)* different? Our Life & Leadership Program is based on spiritual principles that are universal and effective.

Like *Wisdom In New Dimensions (WIND)*, we want you and/or your organization to greatly benefit from the invaluable insight gained through the OLI Life & Leadership Program, therefore we would like you to visit our web site and learn more about us:

www.windinc.org

Partners In Goodwill

Publications & Media

What Inspiration Sounds and Looks Like.

Books, Music, Multi-Media, Creative Print Designs, Writing and Publishing

www.partnersingoodwill.com

Public Speaking & Book Signings

www.danarondel.com

*The Book of Life
Affirmative Notes To Self*

Written by You

May the power of your spirit, thoughts of your mind, emotions of your heart, feelings of your body and the instrument in your hand produce for you, on the next pages, words that will become your life, beautiful, harmonious, prosperous and peaceful...I wish this for you...

- *Dana Rondel*

◈

◈